Diet and Exercise

Cheryl **Caldwell**

KPT PUBLISHING

Once again, you find yourself dieting.

It's either that or buy new clothes.

That moment you realize your fat pants are now your regular pants, and you need new fat pants.

Which never works out
as we planned.

Apparently there is a reason they call them "skinny jeans" and not "make-you-skinny jeans."

We all know diet alone won't help.

And starving yourself
is no good.

Why must my stomach decide to play "Let-me-sing-the-song-of-my-people" whenever the room grows quiet?

It makes you do crazy things.

My BOSS said my assignment was a piece of cake...

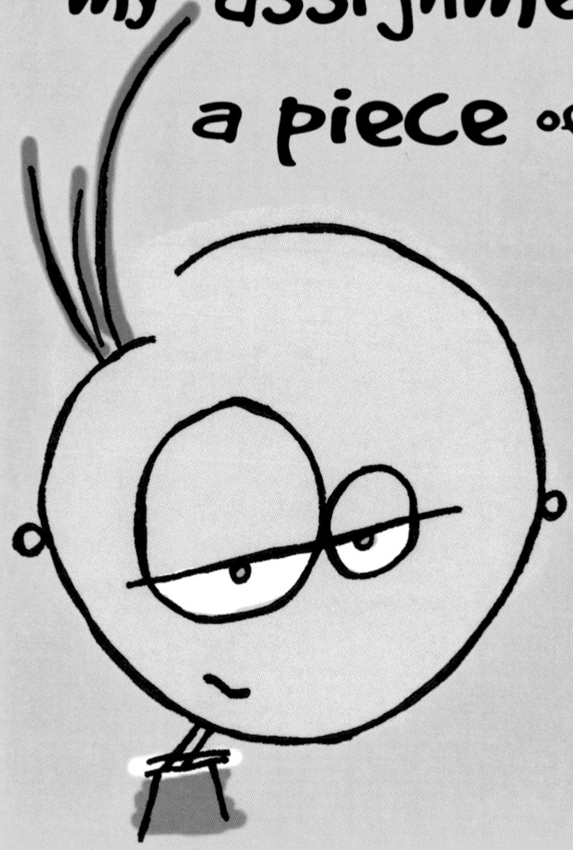

so I ate it.

Not to mention cranky.

You need to exercise
as well.

Which may mean taking
on new endeavors.

So you incorporate
a workout routine

and join groups of
like-minded people.

You set goals.

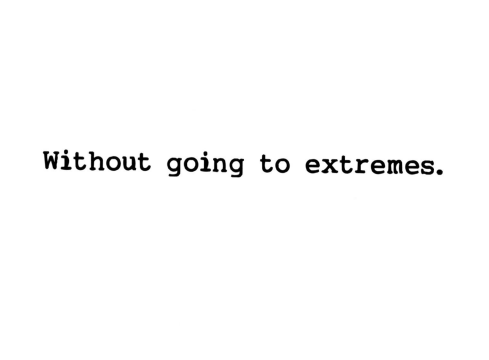

Without going to extremes.

And fit in a bit of exercise
in unlikely places.

I ran into a spider web.
And did a week's worth
of cardio.

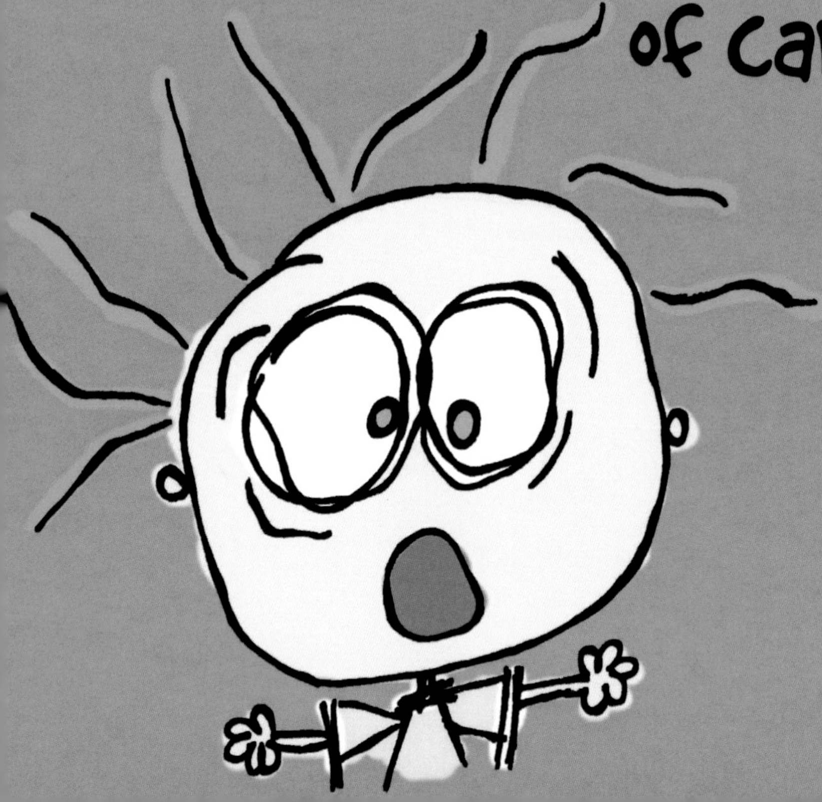

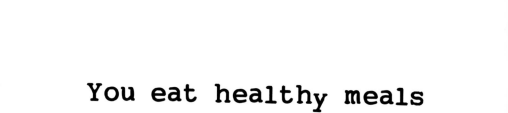

You eat healthy meals

...for the most part.

Open Refrigerator.
Nothing to eat.
Close Refrigerator.
Lower standards.
Repeat.

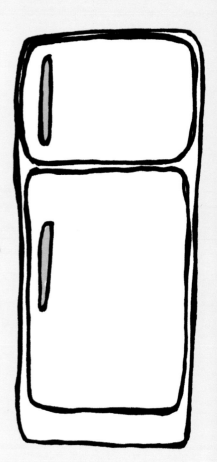

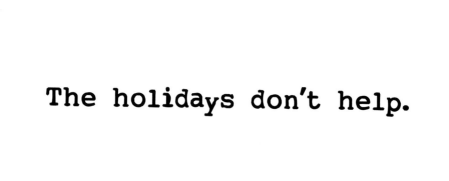

The holidays don't help.

But there will always be setbacks.

So, you can't give up.

Go the Extra Mile: surely someone will find YOU and bring you back!

Even when it feels hopeless.

If someone were to murder me right now, my chalk outline would be a circle.

Of course, a positive body image is also important.

Because in the end,
a thigh gap isn't all
it's cracked up to be.

About the Author

Cheryl Caldwell is a sometimes artist, photographer, filmmaker, marine aquarist, and author. Most of her inspiration comes from her unconventional view of the world and the fact that she finds the mundane hilarious. She is owner of Co-edikit®, a humor-based company that pairs comical illustrations with a witty combination of clear-cut, down-to-earth words of wisdom and sarcastic humor. Her artwork and characters have been licensed and sold throughout the world. Her original paintings of the Co-edikit® characters can be found in several art galleries in the U.S., including Bee Galleries in New Orleans. She still subscribes to the philosophy that if you're having a bad day, ask a four- or five-year-old to skip. It's hysterical.

Diet and Exercise

Copyright © 2018 Cheryl Caldwell

Published by KPT Publishing
Minneapolis, Minnesota 55406
www.KPTPublishing.com

ISBN: 978-1-944833-42-8

Design and production by Koechel Peterson and Associates, Minneapolis, Minnesota

First printing May 2018

10 9 8 7 6 5 4 3 2 1

Printed in the United States of America